SPEAKING *of* COMFORT

A LOOK
AT THE HEIDELBERG CATECHISM

SCOTT HOEZEE

CRC Publications
Grand Rapids, Michigan

We thank Scott Hoezee, minister of preaching and administration at Calvin Christian Reformed Church, Grand Rapids, Michigan, for writing this book.

Cover photo: © PhotoDisc, Inc.

Unless otherwise indicated, the Scripture quotations in this publication are from the HOLY BIBLE, NEW INTERNATIONAL VERSION, © 1973, 1978, 1984, International Bible Society. Used by permission of Zondervan Bible Publishers.

Speaking of Comfort: A Look at the Heidelberg Catechism, © 1998 by CRC Publications, 2850 Kalamazoo Ave. SE, Grand Rapids, MI 49560.

All rights reserved. With the exception of brief excerpts for review purposes, no part of this book may be reproduced in any manner whatsoever without written permission from the publisher.

Printed in the United States of America on recycled paper. ♻
1-800-333-8300

Library of Congress Cataloging-in-Publication Data
Hoezee, Scott, 1964-
    Speaking of comfort: a look at the Heidelberg catechism / Scott Hoezee.
        p. cm.
    ISBN 1-56212-376-9 (alk. paper)
    1. Heidelberger Katechismus. 2. Reformed Church—Catechisms—History and criticism. I. Title
BX9428.H64   1998
238'.42—dc21   98-43269
                                                            CIP

10 9 8 7 6 5 4 3 2 1

CONTENTS

Acknowledgments 4

Introduction 5

Unit 1:   Questions Need Answers 7

Unit 2:   The Diagnosis 17

Unit 3:   The Mystery of Grace 27

Unit 4:   Signs and Seals 37

Unit 5:   The Dilemma of Grace 47

Unit 6:   Grateful Requests 57

ACKNOWLEDGMENTS

So much of what I say and write—as well as the way I try to express it—can ultimately be traced back to the influence of Neal Plantinga, my teacher, mentor, and friend. In my years at Calvin Theological Seminary, Neal's sparkling lectures taught me the value of precise yet creative theological thinking as well as the elegance of well-crafted words and carefully chosen illustrations. Anyone who has heard Neal preach or speak or who has read his many wonderful articles and books knows what I mean.

Hence, in most everything I do, I owe Neal a debt of gratitude. In this particular project, however, all of that gets magnified several times. Nearly two decades ago, Neal, while completing his doctoral work at Princeton Seminary, composed an extremely helpful study on the ecumenical creeds and Reformed confessions entitled *A Place to Stand.* This current study is based squarely on that original book—indeed, it is essentially a reworking of it. Although I have reshaped and reshuffled some of the material, and although many of the illustrations are new, the core of this study remains very much the fruit of Neal's original research, work, and good writing.

As always, if there are deficits in this current study, they are wholly my fault. However, most of what is good in the pages ahead must be credited ultimately to Neal. My thanks to him also for asking me to be the writer for this revision and for the encouragement he gave as he peeked at various drafts of this work.

—Scott Hoezee

INTRODUCTION

In his preface to *Speaking as One: A Look at the Ecumenical Creeds,* Cornelius Plantinga, Jr., noted that the creeds of the church are like a dictionary that teaches Christians their first language. The creeds enable us to "talk Christian" by giving us the correct vocabulary for speaking intelligently about God, creation, and the relationship between the two. Similarly, this volume on the Heidelberg Catechism helps us to learn the specific Christian dialect of the Reformed tradition. But notice: this is a *dialect* of the larger Christian language, not a new language altogether.

After all, if a woman who speaks only French finds herself in an elevator with a man who speaks only Russian, there will be very little conversation—indeed, most attempts to communicate will end in confusion and frustration. However, if a British woman finds herself in an elevator with a man from Alabama, then conversation is possible. The inflections of the Queen's English sound very different from the twang of the Deep South, but both parties are speaking English. True, there may be a little translation needed between London and Mobile, but even this will be accomplished with relative ease.

Everyone speaks with an accent. Of course, as a young boy growing up in the American Midwest, I assumed that only *other* people spoke English with an accent! We who lived in Michigan were the ones who spoke straight English—an accent, I thought, was something you heard only in New Jersey or Texas. But when I heard a British woman do an uncannily good imitation of *my* Midwestern accent, I realized the truth.

All Christians speak the same basic theological language, but all Christians do so with an accent. The Heidelberg Catechism is among the world's best summary documents for gaining access to the *Reformed* way of talking. It is a dialect of the faith that we who are Reformed should want to know about, embrace, and cherish as our own.

Some years ago I met an American who had lived in England for a few months. After returning home, he spoke with an English accent, claiming that he had picked it up simply by living there. Of course, everyone knew he was faking it to look like a sophisticated world traveler. He no longer seemed genuinely himself.

So also with the faith: we Reformed Christians have an accent that is our particular contribution to the richness of the Christian language worldwide. We need to be genuinely ourselves by clearly articulating our particular dialect. This study of the Catechism is designed to help us catch the twang of the Reformed faith in the hope that this understanding will make us better communicators with our Christian brothers and sisters around the world.

—Scott Hoezee

UNIT ONE

QUESTIONS NEED ANSWERS

No sooner are children able to form words and sentences than they begin to ask questions. Children are naturally inquisitive about everything they see, hear, taste, and experience. Asking questions is how children explore their world; receiving answers is how they come to understand their world.

Catechisms try to tap into this natural rhythm of experience and learning by asking questions that the authors hope will interest their readers. The authors then provide the biblical answers to those questions. Indeed, the word *catechism* comes from the Greek word *catecheo*, which means "to pass down information." The answers contained in a catechism are designed to be as enduringly biblical as possible so that they will be passed down from generation to generation.

Of course, no catechism could anticipate every question that a religious seeker might ask (and every catechism will contain a few questions that some people would *never* ask).

In our day of radical individualism many people shun catechisms. Some people claim that any document so old must be hopelessly outdated and irrelevant. Some are interested only in contemporary expressions of faith and worship that are tailored to people's current tastes and preferences. The way a catechism predetermines the issues to be addressed may offend some ("I want *my* questions answered, not ones that someone came up with four centuries ago!"). Many people in North America today are suspicious of prepackaged truths, preferring to discover their own "truth" as it is formed from and validated by their own personal experiences—whatever "works" for them.

A catechism anticipates the questions a religious seeker might ask, but it also demonstrates the kinds of questions one *should* ask. This does not mean that the Heidelberg Catechism is exhaustive. Nor does it deny that some very important questions simply do not appear among its 129 questions and answers.

In a day of narcissism and radical individualism, we need to admit that personal taste and preference are not always reliable guides. People who have questions about life and religion do not necessarily ask the right questions. Catechisms remind us that sometimes we need to be taught both the right questions and the right way to ask them.

Education seeks to expose children to new areas of learning and to stimulate them to ask questions they would never ask on their own. Likewise, the Heidelberg Catechism attempts to expose readers to the full range of the Bible's concerns and so stimulate in them the right kinds of questions.

As we open this study of the Heidelberg Catechism, let's begin with a brief recap of the Catechism's history and a look at its memorable opening lines.

Is the Q & A format dead? Not a chance! Check almost any magazine from *Christianity Today* to *Mad* to the Ann Landers column in the daily newspaper. Somewhere you'll find a Question and Answer column. They're so popular because, when done well, they connect with our personal desire to know. They provide answers to questions we wanted to ask, but didn't know how. Or maybe we did ask the questions and we even answered them, but when the questions popped out at us from the page, we couldn't wait to see how someone else answered them—that's what makes the Heidelberg Catechism so intriguing. It asks the intensely personal questions that lie deep within our souls.

HOME AWAY FROM HOME

North Americans who tour Europe are often struck by the rich antiquity of the places they visit, in part because it stands in such sharp contrast to North America. If, for instance, you tour the Midwest of the United States, you may occasionally see a historical marker announcing that a certain farm is a

"Centennial Farm," meaning that it has been in the possession of the same family for at least a hundred years. Such a designation may seem significant until you discover buildings in Europe dating back to the ninth century.

Precisely because of its age, almost every European nation, city, town, and village has a rich history. Touring such places gives one a sense of other people's history. There is, however, one European city which, although thousands of miles from North America, feels oddly like home for Reformed Christians who visit it. The German city of Heidelberg is the birthplace of what is perhaps the most widely used of all Reformed confessions of faith: the Heidelberg Catechism.

For more than four hundred years, Reformed churches have found the style and content of "the Heidelberger" to be an excellent resource for training people in the knowledge of the Christian faith as it is filtered through the Reformed tradition. When walking the ramparts of the Heidelberg Castle or sitting in a pew of Heidelberg's Holy Spirit Church, many Reformed Christians have the curious feeling that this place is a part of them.

And it is. Generations of pastors have used the Catechism as a guide for preaching. Generations of believers have heard Catechism sermons and have studied and memorized the Catechism in church school classes. Something of the Catechism has been woven into the fabric of their souls, and its language has influenced their understanding of the Christian faith.

Christians who feel such a historical connection to Heidelberg also have a connection to one of Europe's most significant events: the Protestant Reformation. Sparked by Martin Luther's protest against the Roman Church—as summarized in his ninety-five theses, which he affixed to the door of Wittenberg's City Church on October 31, 1517—the Reformation soon swept across Europe as both a religious and a political movement.

In sixteenth-century Europe there was no disentangling religion from politics. Indeed, the political leaders of the day were all but forced to take sides either for the Roman Catholic Church and against the Protestant Reformation or vice versa. Any leader who decided to be pro-Protestant had his work cut

> Williston Walker wonders how Luther's ninety-five theses could actually spark the Reformation. They were academic. They did not challenge the pope's authority to grant indulgences. They assumed that the pope would want to agree with the theses and stop the abuses they pointed out. But Walker answers his own question: "Certain principles are evident in them which, if developed, would be revolutionary . . . repentance is not an act, but a lifelong habit of mind. The true treasury of the church is God's forgiving grace. The Christian seeks rather than avoids divine discipline. 'Every Christian who feels true compunction has of right plenary remission of pain and guilt, even without letter of pardon'" (*A History of the Christian Church*, Third Edition, p. 305). Here we detect the faint heartbeat of the faith that is so fully fleshed out in the Heidelberg Catechism.

out for him. He had to defend himself and his people against papal charges of heresy—charges that could have the gravest consequences. He also had to educate his people about the biblical and theological interpretations of Reformers like Martin Luther in Germany, Ulrich Zwingli in Switzerland, and John Calvin in France.

A common way to accomplish both these tasks was to compose confessions of faith or catechisms. Certainly that was the goal of Elector Frederick III. From 1559 to 1576, Frederick was the prince in charge of the German state of the Palatinate, whose capital city was Heidelberg. In the wake of Luther's protests—and the break from the Catholic Church that those protests ultimately caused—sixteenth-century Germany saw many religious and political battles over who was permitted to believe what. The controversies were finally resolved in 1555 through a political-religious treaty known as the Peace of Augsburg. This agreement officially allowed Germans a choice: the law would permit them to embrace either Roman Catholicism or Lutheranism.

As a key leader in Germany—and as one of seven European rulers who elected the emperor of the entire Holy Roman Empire—Frederick III was expected to follow the law of the land, including the Peace of Augsburg. But Frederick's piety leaned neither toward Roman Catholicism nor toward Lutheranism. Frederick's beliefs were much more in sympathy with the teachings of the Swiss reformer Zwingli and the French reformer John Calvin (who by that time was living in Geneva, having fled his native France). Indeed, when Calvin published the final edition of his landmark *Institutes of the Christian Religion* in 1559, he initially intended to dedicate it to Frederick III but was persuaded not to do so because of the political trouble it would cause Frederick.

Frederick eventually got into trouble on his own. Because he authorized a catechism that turned out to be so clearly flavored with the thought of Calvin (and, at certain points, in opposition to Luther's teachings), Frederick ultimately had to defend himself in court. Still, despite the political danger to himself, Frederick wanted a teaching tool that could give the people of the Palatinate the essentials of the faith as he himself believed it should be taught. Thus, Frederick commissioned the composition of what became known as the Palatinate or the Heidelberg Catechism.

The Catechism appears to have been written by the theological faculty from the University of Heidelberg. Two men have traditionally been identified as the principal authors: Zacharias Ursinus (1534-1583) and Caspar Olevianus (1536-1587). Ursinus was a teacher at the university and Olevianus was Frederick's handpicked choice to be the pastor of Heidelberg's Holy Spirit Church.

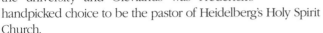

Commissioned to compose a new catechism in early 1562, Ursinus, Olevianus, and their colleagues produced the Heidelberg Catechism in less than a year. Following its approval by a local synod, the first edition of the Heidelberger was published on January 19, 1563. Though it would go through several revisions and become a political flash point for Frederick, the Heidelberg Catechism was quickly embraced for its clear biblical teachings and its warmhearted tone. More than four hundred years later, believers around the world continue to study this Catechism for those same reasons.

THE COMFORT OF DEPENDENCE

The opening words of a catechism may say much about what it intends to teach. For instance, Martin Luther's Small Catechism sets a very moral tone by beginning with an explication of the Ten Commandments. The Anglican Catechism attempts to make its message as personal as possible by asking in its first question, "What is your name?" The Westminster Shorter Catechism sets a cosmic backdrop when it begins with the grand question, "What is the chief end of man?"

The Heidelberger immediately sets a pastoral tone when it asks, "What is your only comfort in life and in death?" From that point forward, the Heidelberg Catechism continues to be warmly personal, pastorally sensitive, and deeply comforting. Indeed, although the word "comfort" occurs only six times in the Catechism, it is clear that the entire document is designed to assure believers of their share in God's salvation through Christ.

The key disagreement between Luther and Calvin centered on the presence of Christ in the Lord's Supper. The church of Rome taught that Christ was made present in the sacrament when the priest blessed the elements, turning them into the actual body and blood of Christ. Reformers like Zwingli taught that the Lord's Supper is only a remembrance of what Christ did for believers on the cross. Luther and Calvin stood between these extremes, but still did not agree. Luther taught that Christ was present in the Supper because the elements of bread and wine participated in his glorified body. Calvin took exception to that view. His teaching is clearly expressed in the Catechism: "The bread of the Lord's Supper is not changed into the actual body of Christ even though it is called the body of Christ . . . [Christ] wants to assure us, by this visible sign and pledge, that we, through the Holy Spirit's work, share in his true body and blood as surely as our mouths receive these holy signs in his remembrance . . ." (Q&A 78, 79).

For instance, in a day when death came swiftly and regularly—recall that the Black Plague had killed up to three-quarters of all Europeans only two hundred years earlier—the original students of the Heidelberg Catechism were assured that gospel comfort extends into and beyond death. In a day when the medieval church used the final judgment as a club to bash people into frightened submission, the Heidelberger scandalously asks, "How does Christ's return 'to judge the living and the dead' comfort you?"

Although a catechism may seem to be aimed only at one's head, the Heidelberg Catechism also aims at the heart. Along with *comfort*, the words *assurance* and *joy* occur often, particularly in those questions and answers that address the Christian faith and the utter assurance provided by that faith through the love of Jesus Christ the Lord.

> Even in our own prosperous times Lord's Day 1 still speaks volumes. Notice that Q&A 1 adds the words "and in death." This explains how we can still speak of only *one* comfort when we have so many comforts. In life we have easy chairs, chocolate fudge, and channel changers. Death, however, steals them all away and narrows all these comforts down to a single one.

What is the source of this comfort and assurance? It comes, the Heidelberg Catechism makes clear, from the Bible alone. The Heidelberg Catechism takes great pains to demonstrate the depth of its biblical roots. One of the main requests that Elector Frederick made of Ursinus and Olevianus was that their work be biblical. Frederick wanted everyone to know that the faith he embraced, and which he desired his people to embrace, sprang directly from God's Word.

In time, the 129 questions and answers of the Heidelberg Catechism were buttressed by 361 footnotes that direct readers to nearly 900 passages of Scripture—an average of seven Bible passages per question and answer!

Because the Bible's story of redemption climaxes in Jesus Christ, the Catechism also is a Christ-centered document. Approximately half of the questions and answers deal directly with some aspect of Christ as the Bible reveals him—indeed, the title "Christ" occurs more than one hundred times.

OUTLINE AND STRUCTURE

In order to deliver its comforting and assuring message of salvation through Christ clearly, the Heidelberg Catechism is divided into three sections, each of which flows naturally into the next.

Following the prologue (Q&A's 1-2), the first section deals with our "Misery" in sin. This brief section (Q&A's 3-11) essentially diagnoses the illness to be cured. The second (and much longer) section (Q&A's 12-85) details our "Deliverance" through Christ. The first section diagnoses our problem as sin; the second section presents the divine cure of faith in Jesus Christ. As a way to flesh out the content of this saving faith, the authors dissect the Apostles' Creed line by line and also present the meaning of the sacraments. The final section (Q&A's 86-129) details how we are to show our "Gratitude" to God for this great deliverance. The two components of the last section are the Ten Commandments and the Lord's Prayer, each of which is analyzed line by line to show how praying and following God's law are ways to thank God for his salvation.

In the next five units we will explore each of these three sections. As we do so, we will observe the theme of comfort even as we allow this historic document to help us form the right questions in the right way. Only by asking the right questions can we hope to receive the answers we need for salvation.

As we will see in the next unit, we need help. God has graciously provided the Word to help us. We also believe that through the Holy Spirit's work in the church, the Heidelberg Catechism has been given to help us grasp the essence of God's Word in ways that are deeply comforting, utterly assuring, and profoundly joyful.

REFLECTIONS

The "Reflections" section of each unit is designed to reinforce what you read. The "Points to Ponder" are suitable for use in a class or small group setting. Group members may take turns reading selections and proposing an explanation before inviting other participants to add thoughts. The questions in the "Implications and Applications" section may be used for group discussion or for personal reflection.

▶ *Points to Ponder*

Education seeks to expose children to new areas of learning and to stimulate them to ask questions they would never ask on their own. Likewise, the Heidelberg Catechism attempts to expose readers to the full range of the Bible's concerns and so stimulate in them the right kinds of questions.

For more than four hundred years, Reformed churches have found the style and content of "the Heidelberger" to be an excellent resource for training people in the knowledge of the Christian faith as it is filtered through the Reformed tradition.

The Heidelberger immediately sets a pastoral tone when it asks, "What is your only comfort in life and in death?" From that point forward, the Heidelberg Catechism continues to be warmly personal, pastorally sensitive, and deeply comforting.

The Heidelberg Catechism takes great pains to demonstrate the depth of its biblical roots. One of the main requests that Elector Frederick made of Ursinus and Olevianus was that their work be biblical.

Because the Bible's story of redemption climaxes in Jesus Christ, the Catechism also is a Christ-centered document. Approximately half of the questions and answers deal directly with some aspect of Christ as the Bible reveals him—indeed, the title "Christ" occurs more than one hundred times.

▶ *Implications and Applications*
1. Why might a question-and-answer format be a good way to "pass down information"?
2. The author suggests some reasons why people shun catechisms today. What other reasons might be added to the list? Are any of these reasons valid? Why or why not?
3. Why is it important for a catechism to teach us to ask the right questions? Why might a person not ask the right questions? What danger is there in asking the wrong questions?
4. Generations of believers have heard the Heidelberg Catechism preached and taught from early childhood. If you grew up with the Heidelberg Catechism, how has it shaped your faith?
5. What do you hope to gain from this study of the Heidelberger?

UNIT
TWO

THE
DIAGNOSIS

In 1986, the world watched in horror as the Chernobyl nuclear power plant suffered a catastrophic meltdown. Believed by many to have been caused in part by an inept and corrupt communist system, Chernobyl spewed radiation into the atmosphere, leaked nuclear heavy water into rivers and streams, and contaminated soil for miles around. Today, residents of that region of Russia are still forced to eat radioactive vegetables and drink contaminated milk and water. Hence, they are seeing a 40 percent spike in cancers of all kinds, including once-rare forms. Thousands die each year in this sector from diseases which, most doctors believe, can be traced directly to the Chernobyl fiasco.

Shortly after the Chernobyl accident someone noticed that the Russian word *chernobyl* is the same word used to translate "wormwood" in the Russian version of Revelation 8:10-11, which speaks of sin's terrible curse on this world: "[A]nd a great star, blazing like a torch, fell from the sky on a third of the rivers and on the springs of water—the name of this star is Wormwood [Bitterness] . . . and many people died from the waters that had become bitter."

Whatever one makes of this odd verbal connection, few would deny that the Chernobyl accident is a tragic vignette of sin and its consequences for our world. Life on planet Earth has become an often bitter reality. Starvation, civil war, drive-by shootings, cancer, drug addiction, divorce, child abuse, assassination, murder, ethnic cleansing, abortion: these are just a few of the headline items that contribute to our world's sorrows. Many people live much of their lives in abject misery, and most people experience misery at least some of the time.

This world's misery can be seen in the sunken eyes of AIDS patients, in the wide-eyed terror etched on the faces of Rwandan refugees or residents of Sarajevo. Misery is visible everywhere. But though much of this world's misery is easy to identify—indeed, much of life's misery is impossible to miss—the Catechism knows that the worst misery of all can easily go undetected.

It is possible to be healthy, wealthy, successful, and comfortable and still be utterly miserable. As Part I of the Heidelberg Catechism makes clear, humanity's deepest misery is being disconnected from the Creator. In the long run no condition could be more dire than alienation from the one who is our source and destiny.

The Bible teaches, and the Catechism reflects, that sin blinds us to our estrangement from God. We were created in the image of God both to reflect God to one another and to glorify him in the conduct of our lives. We were made to live in God's world, breathing the atmosphere of God's Spirit. But sin obscures this reality, making us comfortable with being our own masters in little worlds of our own devising.

The Catechism's authors used the German word for "misery," which is *Elend*. The root meaning of this word is "to be out of one's native land." Just as Adam and Eve were cast out of Eden, so all humanity has been cast out of its true country. We were designed for fellowship with our Creator God, but sin has made us outcasts and refugees. Having become accustomed to a fallen world, many people are blinded to this reality.

> In *Comfort and Joy: A Study of the Heidelberg Catechism,* Andrew Kuyvenhoven agrees with this sobering assessment: "The trouble with most people is that they don't know the trouble we are in. Therefore their proposed solutions make no sense. One cannot prescribe a cure before one has diagnosed the illness" (p. 17).

At the end of C. S. Lewis's *Chronicles of Narnia*, Aslan the Lion—the Christ-figure of these stories—draws Narnia's history to a close and brings into existence the New Narnia, the heavenly paradise of the New Creation.

But in the midst of the New Narnia's mind-numbing wonders, beauties, and glories, a group of dwarves is huddled together, despising all they see, hear, taste, and smell. They are given a luscious delicacy of the New Narnia only to gag on it as if it were cow dung. When they are presented with the loveliest flower anyone had ever beheld, they jump back from it, sensing only a vile-smelling thistle. They sit in the bright light of the New Narnia's sun but see only the darkness of an old stable.

Aslan explains by telling the others that the dwarves had become prisoners of their own minds. They grew so accustomed to the dim world of the Old Narnia that they couldn't recognize the wild goodness of the New Narnia.

We also live in an inverted world in which many people have no ear for God's tunes and no taste for God's nourishing presence. Unhappily, this chief misery of human existence cannot always be detected. Just as a man may feel perfectly healthy while cancer devours his pancreas, so some of the happiest and most successful people live in a state of spiritual misery, having lost their connection to God.

The Heidelberg Catechism provides a kind of spiritual CAT scan—an MRI for our spirits. The Catechism's first section scans the human soul and reveals a large, deadly tumor. We've fallen away from what we were created to be. We've fallen away from our Creator's intentions for us. And he is not pleased. Unless something is done to cure this disease, we are sick unto death—eternal death.

> We can describe our miserable human condition before God as alienation and terminal illness. What other ways can you think of to describe it? What images does the Bible use?

BRIEF BUT DEVASTATING

If you've ever had a CAT scan or an MRI, then you know the agony of waiting for test results. You also know the awful expectancy that comes as you await the doctor's arrival to deliver the news. If the doctor steps into the room with a light step, grim expectancy gives way to cautious ecstasy. But if the doctor is oddly quiet and a bit hesitant, your heart sinks, weighted by fear and dread.

Although Calvinists are often lampooned as people who morbidly dwell on sin and guilt, it is curious to note that the Catechism's segment on our sinful misery is the briefest part of this document. This first section has only nine questions and answers (as opposed to seventy-seven questions and answers in section two and forty-four in section three), and some of these answers are among the briefest in the Catechism.

Still, there is little doubt that this section is meant to make us uncomfortable. A serious student of the Catechism is supposed to feel discomfort upon reading these words. The test results of our spiritual MRI are in, and the doctor's manner is anything but sprightly as he settles in to discuss the news with us.

How does this spiritual scan accomplish its task? It illuminates our soul with the waves of God's law. "How do you come to know your sin and misery? The law of God tells me" (Q&A 3). Note that the Catechism does not invoke the specifics of the Ten Commandments but rather gives Jesus' summary of the law from Matthew 22. This was a strategic move by the authors.

Jesus' "law of love" summary cuts to the heart of every one of us. Had the Catechism included the Ten Commandments at this point, readers may have treated those laws like a checklist for external behavior. Such a list may have allowed people to feel as if they were not so bad off. "I haven't made any graven images, stolen anything, committed adultery, murdered . . . I guess I'm not so bad after all—I'm a pretty good person."

But Jesus' summary of the law reminds us what it's all about: an unflagging and perfect love of God's person as well as of his full desire for this Creation, which includes an undying love for our neighbors (which, as Jesus also made clear in his ministry, includes everybody we meet). Put this way, it is much harder to let ourselves off God's hook. If perfect love is what God's law is all about, then we fall short every time. And if perfection is what God asks of us in order to maintain fellowship with him, then we are finished.

The Catechism leaves no doubt that we are indeed washed up, morally speaking. Its language is unstintingly blunt and even harsh. Can we live up to God's law of love? No, we naturally hate God and everybody else. Are we so bad off that we don't do any good? Yes, we are altogether corrupt. What happens to people like us unless something changes? We go to hell.

In these brief strokes the Catechism is intentionally bracing and shocking. It shuts every door that might allow us to think that the solution to sin can be achieved by our own efforts. The picture is utterly bleak. But it is this very bleakness that makes us desperately hungry to devour God's salvation once it is shown to us.

Before we identify the origins of this predicament, perhaps a few qualifying statements about the Catechism's language are in order. Many people, upon reading Q&A 8's words about our inability to do any good, wonder where that leaves the undeniably good and generous acts done by many of the non-Christians in our world. The doctrine of common grace teaches that a remnant of God's image remains in all people to the extent that even non-Christians are able to do many right, good, moral, and uplifting things.

Does the Catechism intend to deny this doctrine? No. Perhaps we could properly nuance Q&A 8 were we to add the adjective "saving" in front of the word "good." "Are we able to do any *saving* good—any works that by themselves will restore us to full fellowship with our Creator God?" The answer remains no. All that people do—even their noblest actions—is tainted. Praiseworthy though such deeds may be, no such act can ever admit a person into God's kingdom.

Although our misery began on the human side of things, the solution to it cannot come from our side. We are trapped in a vicious cycle of sin from which we cannot escape. Each day we dig the hole a little deeper. We are in a most desperate fix.

> It's been often said that Calvinist Christians believe so much in total depravity that they can't stop living that way. But notice that the grim reality of our total corruption is what we *were,* not what we *are* or shall be. When Q&A 8 asks "Are we so corrupt that we are totally unable to do any good and inclined toward all evil?" it responds with a very firm "Yes . . ." But the answer does not stop there, it continues: ". . . *unless* we are born again, by the Spirit of God."

ORIGINS

The Catechism sets up this predicament in pithy sentences. Then, in equally brief strokes, it identifies the source of our dismal corruption and woe: our first parents, Adam and Eve. Their fall into sin affected the whole of their posterity. Some kind of link exists between each of us and that first couple. (The Catechism provides no more explanation of how this works than does the Bible itself.)

Throughout history, theologians have searched for a metaphor to communicate this link. Some have pictured a tree drawing disease from the soil, which results in the spread of the disease through every limb, branch, twig, and leaf of the tree. Others have envisioned humanity as a polluted stream resulting from sludge poured in at the head of the river. Modern theologians have speculated about genetic links, as if sin kinked Adam and Eve's DNA strand in ways that are replicated with each succeeding child.

Whatever image we choose, the point is the same: all people are born sinners. We do not become sinners when we commit a sin for the first time; we commit sin because we were born that way. Few parents think of their cherubic babies as troublemakers, thieves, or liars. But the truth is that children are just like mom and dad: they are sinners who will grow up to commit sins—big sins and little sins, scandalous sins and mundane sins.

As author Garry Wills once put it, human history is "a linked series of disasters . . . we are hostages of a deadly interrelatedness. At one time a woman of unsavory enough experience was delicately but cruelly referred to as 'having a past.' The doctrine of original sin states that humankind, in exactly that sense, 'has a past.'" And so we do.

By God's grace we also have a future—a future for which this first section of the Catechism makes us eager. The profound discomfort of this section is a setup to make us snuggle all the more luxuriously into the utter comfort of the Catechism's gospel summary.

Is it fair that we inherited this sinful condition from Adam and Eve? Kuyvenhoven observes: "We bristle in self-defense: That temptation happened to Adam and Eve. It happened millennia ago. Why should we be doomed for what none of us remembers? Here again it's a matter of perspective. We protest like individualists. But the Bible says that the very fact that we are able to think of ourselves as unrelated, disunited individuals presents evidence of our sinful perspective. God's revelation views the human race not as a pile of gravel but as a giant tree. We are not pebbles thrown together but twigs and branches on a tree, all organically united" (p. 32).

NO PAIN, NO GAIN

The Catechism's authors recognized a fact that many people seem to miss: acknowledging our sin is clarifying and reassuring. To return to our medical analogy, there are few things in life as unpleasant as a medical mystery. No one wants to be what doctors call "an interesting case."

Some people are forced to spend weeks or months shuttling from one specialist to the next, only to find in each office a head-scratching uncertainty about what is wrong. For people like this, a diagnosis is a relief. Provided the diagnosis is not "incurable," receiving the definitive word can be a good thing: now something can be done.

Medical mysteries are no fun, but neither are spiritual ones. Though many people may not be aware of the exact contours of their miserable state, they do sense that something is out of joint. Many such folks try various self-help cures—they try to slake their inner spiritual thirst at all the wrong taps: sex, alcohol, drugs, money, travel, prestige. In the end many discover only a deepened thirst for meaning and so they keep wondering, What is wrong? What is missing?

For such people the Catechism's swift and definitive diagnosis is good, albeit discomfiting. Such a diagnosis offers the possibility of treatment. In this case it offers the good gospel news that something *already* has been done. It is that "something"—indeed, it is finally a certain "Someone"—to which the Catechism turns in its section on "Deliverance."

In recent years, it has been deemed improper and unpopular for churches to speak of sin. Modern people do not want to be depressed by sin and guilt. Rather, they want their self-esteem enhanced, the shine on their egos buffed to a high sheen. For people such as this, Part I of the Heidelberg Catechism may seem quaintly offensive.

Assuming that one could accept the scandal of Q&A 1 and its message that we are not our own but belong completely to Another, it seems unlikely that many modern readers could get past Q&A's 3-11 without setting the entire Catechism aside. In reality, the Catechism's second and third sections are unnecessary—even intrusive—if the truths of the "Misery" section are not known and accepted. Without a full disclosure of our sin

In Lord's Day 1 the Catechism has anticipated the only answer to our desperate situation. It's not just a theoretical one, but a deeply personal one. Our abiding comfort rests not in a thought or a drug, but in a relationship. Fred Klooster points out: "The first question and answer of the Heidelberg Catechism is intensely personal. The question asks: 'What is *your* only comfort in life and in death?' The answer states: '*I* am not *my* own, but belong . . . to *my* faithful Savior Jesus Christ.' This is another remarkable feature of this little Catechism. From beginning to end, it is a warm, personal profession of faith. The questions are asked of the *believer;* the answers are framed in such a way that only one who truly believes can utter them" *(A Mighty Comfort,* p. 14).

and misery, there is precious little from which we need God to deliver us. Without the hellish discomfort of this section we will never fully celebrate the heavenly comfort of what follows.

If you have a cold, you may be grateful for a lozenge to soothe your scratchy throat, but that is a small-scale gratitude. As annoying as the common cold may be, it's still just a cold and it will pass. However, a terminally ill person experiences true gratitude when he or she hears that a surefire cure has been discovered. Death will not come; the illness will be completely eradicated. It is this kind of gratitude that the Catechism hopes to kindle in us. Only those who do not throw the Catechism aside at this point will come to understand true gratitude.

REFLECTIONS

▶ *Points to Ponder*

Life on planet Earth has become an often bitter reality. Starvation, civil war, drive-by shootings, cancer, drug addiction, divorce, child abuse, assassination, murder, ethnic cleansing, abortion: these are just a few of the headline items that contribute to our world's sorrows.

It is possible to be healthy, wealthy, successful, and comfortable and still be utterly miserable.

The test results of our spiritual MRI are in, and the doctor's manner is anything but sprightly as he settles in to discuss the news with us.

All that people do—even their noblest actions—is still tainted. Praiseworthy though such deeds may be, no such act can ever admit a person into God's kingdom.

All people are born sinners. We do not become sinners when we commit a sin for the first time; we commit sin because we were born that way.

In recent years, it has been deemed improper and unpopular for churches to speak of sin. Modern people do not want to be depressed by sin and guilt.

▶ *Implications and Applications*

1. "Sin has made us outcasts and refugees," the author writes. How have you seen that to be true in your own experience?

2. How does the Heidelberg Catechism serve as "an MRI for our spirits"? What does it reveal?

3. Why should the Ten Commandments not be regarded as a checklist for external behavior?

4. How can acknowledging our sin be reassuring?

5. Why is the "Misery" section (Q&A's 3-11) of the Catechism so necessary?

THE MYSTERY OF GRACE

In the film *Tender Mercies* Robert Duvall plays Mac, a one-time country-western singing star whose life has dissolved into a fog of alcohol and aimlessness. Divorced from his wife, estranged from his only daughter, and no longer sober enough to write or record music, Mac lurches through life until one day he collapses in a stupor on the porch of a small gas station on the Texas prairie. The station is run by a kindly young widow and her ten-year-old son. They take Mac in and, with gentle prodding and low-key encouragement, help him to kick his drinking habit. In the course of the film, Mac marries this gentle woman, becomes a sturdy father figure to the little boy, begins to record music again, and is baptized in the local church.

Mac also meets up with his estranged daughter for the first time in many years and begins to build a new relationship with her. Tragically, the daughter dies in a car accident soon after their reunion. Near the end of the film Mac talks to his wife about the mysteries of existence. Speaking in simple, clipped sentences, Mac professes that he doesn't understand a thing about life. It's a mystery to him why he became a drunk and why this woman took him in, helped him, and led him to Christianity. It's a mystery to him why his daughter had to die; it's also a mystery why he has found happiness in his new family. The good and the bad, the beautiful and the ugly, the gracious and the terrible—it all seems equally inexplicable.

People often lament the tragedies of life. "Why do bad things happen to good people?" they ask. But Mac's soliloquy reminds us that good things—God's "tender mercies"—come just as unbidden and surprisingly as do bad and wretched things. Ultimately it is a mystery why some folks receive such goodness when many others live their whole lives in wretched misery. Goodness can catch us off guard just as swiftly as evil can.

Reflecting the keynote of the Reformed tradition, the Heidelberg Catechism declares that the deliverance we receive from sin's misery comes from out of the blue as a divine gift. Certainly we never earn or deserve this gift. In fact, the Catechism takes great pains to explain that people who feel they have earned or deserve salvation prove thereby that they have not received it. God's deliverance comes as a free, unmerited gift or it doesn't come at all.

THE ONLY WAY

The Catechism's "Deliverance" section begins with eight questions and answers (Q&A's 12-19) that pound away at the same uncompromising message emerging from the "Misery" section: namely, we are guilty of a sin whose price and penalty we can never pay ourselves. None of us can solve his or her personal sin problem, let alone help anyone else.

Using an image from the medieval era (and one often used in the Bible as well), the Catechism's authors compare sin to financial debt. Sin means we owe an enormous debt to God. Can we ever pay it off? Can we, on our own, balance the ledger? No. As sinful human beings, we do not have the capi-

---

A maze is challenging because it offers many paths that look right but take us nowhere. In Q&A's 12-19 the Catechism leads us to the only real answer to our quest for salvation by cutting off all the blind alleys. What are some dead-end paths we might take that the Catechism warns us away from?

tal necessary to pay this debt—indeed, we keep falling further behind every day.

Imagine a person who spends far beyond his means by charging everything to a credit card. When the monthly bill comes, he finds he's unable even to come close to paying his balance. Terrifyingly, he also sees that the credit company's eighteen percent compound interest is causing his unpaid balance to increase every day. But far from learning his lesson, the man stupidly keeps putting more charges on the card.

This, the Catechism says, is a snapshot of sin. Humanly speaking, our situation is hopeless. But hopelessness is where we were left after the "Misery" section. So why is the Catechism hammering us with this despairing message again? It is doing so to introduce us to Jesus, the only Being in the universe who can pay our debt for us. Jesus is the full and eternal Son of God and as such (to carry through the financial metaphor), he has infinite wealth. By becoming a human being, Jesus also stands in solidarity with—and is able to help—the indebted party; namely, all human beings.

In quick strokes the Heidelberg Catechism summarizes a great deal of complicated theology. The question of why Jesus had to become human and how his being both human and divine enables him to save us can quickly become confusing. The Catechism boils off most of the dizzying philosophical and theological details simply to say that only someone who is both fully human and fully divine can save humanity. Jesus alone fits the bill.

But how do we hook into the person and work of Jesus? How do the words and deeds of a Jewish carpenter's son from half-way around the world and from over two thousand years ago impact us? What could possibly overcome the geographic, historical, cultural, and temporal distances that separate us from Jesus' ministry and saving work? The answer: Faith.

FAITH ALONE

Novelist Russell Banks described one of his characters this way: "He believes in God the way he believes in politicians—he knows He exists but he doesn't depend on Him for anything." Of course, this sort of belief in God hardly constitutes faith. As the Catechism makes clear, faith involves more than believing certain things—it also involves a complete and comforting dependence on God as a result of those beliefs.

The clarion call of the Reformation centered on faith. Raised to believe he had to pay his own way to heaven, Martin Luther's eyes were wondrously opened when he read the gospel news that "the just shall live by faith . . . for it is by grace that you have been saved through faith." Hence, one of the Reformation's key slogans was "faith alone." Only faith as granted by God can make us right with God. We do not have to pay our own way—it's prepaid by Jesus and gift-wrapped for us in the package of faith.

Given that the Heidelberg Catechism is a premiere Reformation document, it is surprising that only a few brief questions and answers concern faith. Indeed, only one (Q&A 21) directly describes faith. The Catechism appears to spend far more time, for instance, on the sacraments, to which fully eighteen very lengthy questions and answers are dedicated at the end of this second section.

This apparently modest treatment of faith, however, is deceptive. In reality, the bulk of the Catechism is about faith. In addition to Q&A's 20-23, Q&A's 59-64 also address various vital contours of faith and its function for Christians. What's more, the entire explication of the Apostles' Creed (Q&A's 24-58) is an extended description of faith. All told, more than one-third of the Catechism's questions and answers deal with various facets of faith.

So what is faith, according to the Catechism? Q&A 20, though brief, tells us simply that faith in Jesus is what saves us. Faith is the wire that conducts the power of Jesus into our hearts; faith is the pipeline through which the cleansing blood of Jesus flows into our souls; faith is the conduit or channel of communion between Jesus and us. Picking up on one of Jesus' own metaphors, the Catechism tells us that faith is the graft that makes us living branches on the divine trunk of Jesus. Faith patches us directly into Jesus through a living and intimate connection—the "sap" of Jesus now flows into us, helping us to produce lovely spiritual fruit.

In short, if there is no faith, then Jesus remains a distant figure. If a person has no faith, then Jesus might as well be just a man who lived a long time ago and halfway around the world. Although Christians believe that Jesus is alive and reigning in heaven today, the Catechism makes it clear that people who have no faith are no more connected to Jesus than the average person is hooked into, say, Socrates or Lincoln.

Given the vital importance of faith, the next question urgently yet simply asks, "What is true faith?" The answer declares that faith is chiefly two things: knowledge and assurance. Some people seem to believe that a vague and undefined faith is enough; it doesn't matter what you believe as long as you believe in something. To these people, a generic "Higher Power," the New Age "god within yourself," or another form of god is enough to qualify you as a religious person with a bright future.

But the Catechism asserts that true faith is specific—you believe everything God teaches and reveals in the Bible. This specific knowledge births in us a deep-rooted assurance; namely, that God loves us so much that he has taken away the disease and debt of sin fully and freely. We have been saved by "sheer grace" and are assured that no matter how bad we've been or how bad we may be in the future, we will never slip through Jesus' fingers. His grip on us is eternally firm.

Next the Catechism explores the knowledge component of faith by laying out in specific detail the articles of the Apostles' Creed. Note that this section on the Creed is not solely about knowledge. Knowledge and assurance are inseparable. Our assurance, our peace of heart and mind, comes from the ins and outs of biblical and theological knowledge. The Apostles' Creed cannot be adequately studied apart from an awareness of the comfort it brings. Indeed, the careful reader of the Catechism will note how often the authors pause in the midst of explaining some doctrine to ask, "Now then, how does knowing this comfort you?"

RIGHT WITH GOD

Following its lengthy explication of the Apostles' Creed, the Catechism returns to some basic questions about faith

Klooster gives some historical perspective here: "When the Catechism was written, the Roman Catholic Church minimized the assurance of faith. Assurance could be had only by the most saintly people and it came by way of special revelation. Most Christians were kept in doubt and uncertainty; they believed that personal 'good works' and indulgences were required for salvation. In such circumstances assurance was rare. . . . When [the Heidelberg Christians] rediscovered the comfort of the gospel, they also rediscovered the assurance of faith and the security of the believer" (p. 28).

It's appropriate that the Catechism incorporates and enlarges upon the Apostles' Creed. "It took many lifetimes to get this creed fermented, clarified, and aged just right; . . . centuries of agonizing biblical and theological work lie behind even its simplest lines. So we should savor it, especially because the Apostles' Creed presents timeless truths that connect us with our Savior. Sad to say, we often 'gulp' this creed instead. Familiarity breeds contempt" (*Speaking as One*, p. 22).

(Q&A's 59-64). Having expended a great deal of energy digesting the articles of the Creed, a thoughtful Catechism reader may be tempted to ask, "OK, we've covered a lot of ground now as to what we Christians believe. So remind me again, what good does it do to embrace these truths?" The answer is that only this very specific Christian faith makes us "right with God."

Although the Catechism nowhere uses the word "justification"—the theological concept that John Calvin once called "the hinge of the Reformation"—the frequent mention of being made "right with God" is the essence of justification.

Frederick Buechner once explained justification this way: every computer contains various page formats that allow you to arrange the printed text as you wish. You can, for instance, format a document to be double-spaced or single-spaced, in large print or in smaller print, in regular type or boldface, with a one-inch or a two-inch margin.

You also can format a document with left, right, or full justification. If you "right justify" the text, all the words on the right side of the page will line up along the same invisible vertical line. Instead of a jagged effect, the words will stand in a right relationship with the edge of the paper, which is also a straight line. This is called "justification." If a page is justified, there is a corresponding relationship between the words and the edge of the page.

Theologically, being justified means standing in a right relationship with God. There is a "lining up" of our lives with God, our characters with God's character, our conduct with God's law. There are no jagged edges, no obstacles standing between us and a snug relationship with our God. We fit together.

But given how bad off we human beings are—as the Catechism went to grim lengths to prove earlier—how in the world can such a right relationship happen? From our human point of view, the door to that possibility seems closed, locked, bolted, and nailed shut. We do not chip away at our salvation through a series of good deeds that cancel out our bad deeds. We do not pay off our debt on an installment plan. As we said earlier, that can never happen.

"What makes you right with God? Many people rightly see this as the most important question in the world. But their answer to it is dead wrong. They imagine their own good works will put them right with God. They try to gain salvation by jumping through a set of hoops they themselves construct.

"The Bible gives us the answer to this question, an answer so surprising that we would never come up with it on our own. It's an answer that's important to know, to remember, and to share with those who ask the right question but need someone to help them find the right answer" (*Quest of Faith*, p. 21).

No, the solution is grace alone. God does the entire job for us in one fell swoop of mercy. God credits to our account the infinite riches of Christ and so wipes out our debt. God transfers to us the full and stunning righteousness of Jesus and so, when he looks at us he sees only the perfection of Jesus. It's all a gift. It's all free. It's all undeserved.

And yet earlier we said that we are saved by faith. Doesn't our attaining and then holding onto this faith constitute some effort of ours? Is it perhaps that God does most of the work but that our coming to faith is our contribution to the deal? Again, the answer is a resounding "NO!" for even faith is God's gift. True, our faith allows us to grasp and understand God's grace, but his grace is at work in us before we are able to grasp it. By grace God first gives us the container of faith and then, by a further grace, God fills this receptacle with the perfection of Christ.

Think of it this way: faith is the antenna that pulls in and focuses the signals of the gospel picture. Unless God fits us with this antenna in the first place, we will never see the picture. Even as you read these words, television signals are passing in, through, and around you. You do not notice them and cannot create a TV picture in your brain, because you lack the necessary hardware. Only a TV outfitted with an aerial or a cable connection can receive, unscramble, and then project such signals.

The signals of God's grace flood the cosmos. Jesus is the Lord who reigns supreme. Many people don't know this. They hear the message but it passes right through them, leaving no trace of recognition. Only if God comes to us and fits us with the antenna of faith can we understand these truths. Faith is not our work—it is not our contribution to salvation. Rather, the bestowing of faith is itself the first act of God's grace.

As Q&A's 61-63 make clear, nothing we do or could ever do moves us any closer to God or contributes to salvation. It is all gift and all grace from first to last. That's why in the New Testament Paul never allows anyone to say that they are saved by "grace and. . . ." "Grace" is always the first and the last word. It is followed not by a comma but by a period—or better yet, by an exclamation point!

THE WONDER OF IT ALL

We noted above how the character of Mac puzzled over life's hard knocks and God's tender mercies. Unhappily, we Christians often fail to share Mac's sense of wonder. We tend to regard our faith and our Christian lives as proof that we were stellar candidates for God's salvation in the first place. Of course God chose us—how could he not? At some point we may ponder why bad things happen to us but, regrettably, we too seldom are awestruck by the good things, including the chief good of God's grace.

The careful student of the Catechism may find a way to renew this kind of wonder. If you take seriously the Catechism's uncompromising words on sin and misery, then you cannot help but be happily devastated that so horrid a problem could be put away so freely.

If you learn this, then like Mac you will be left scratching your head over the wonder and the mystery of it all. But, also like Mac, you may discover in your heart a gratitude so rich and so deep that words alone cannot express it fully. Rather, such gratitude becomes something you live every single day. The Catechism's concluding section gives us a guide to grateful living. But before we turn to that, let's pause first to consider the Catechism's treatment of the sacraments.

REFLECTIONS

▶ *Points to Ponder*

The Heidelberg Catechism declares that the deliverance we receive from sin's misery comes from out of the blue as a divine gift. Certainly we never earn or deserve this gift. Only faith as granted by God can make us right with God. We do not have to pay our own way—it's prepaid by Jesus and gift-wrapped for us in the package of faith.

Faith is the wire that conducts the power of Jesus into our hearts; faith is the pipeline through which the cleansing blood of Jesus flows into our souls; faith is the conduit or channel of communion between Jesus and us.

Theologically, being justified means standing in a right relationship with God. There is a "lining up" of our lives with God, our characters with God's character, our conduct with God's law.

Our faith allows us to grasp and understand God's grace, but his grace is at work in us before we are able to grasp it. By grace God first gives us the container of faith and then, by a further grace, God fills this receptacle with the perfection of Christ.

"Grace" is always the first and the last word—it is followed not by a comma but by a period—or better yet, by an exclamation point!

▶ *Implications and Applications*

1. How would you answer the question "Why do bad things happen to good people?"

2. Why is Jesus the only one able to redeem sinful people?

3. Define true faith in your own words. How has this unit expanded your understanding of true faith?

4. What are some common things that people put their faith in today?

5. Why can a true believer never say, "I am saved by grace and . . ."? How does "grace and . . ." cheapen the gospel message?

6. How do you respond to the reality of God's grace in your life?

UNIT FOUR

SIGNS AND SEALS

The Catechism's section on the sacraments (the longest section devoted to any one topic) highlights the acute controversy that surrounded the sacraments in the Reformation era. In the sixteenth century, Protestants and Catholics sparred with one another over the number of sacraments (the Catholics claimed seven, the Protestants two) and particularly over the Lord's Supper.

But controversy over the sacraments was not limited to skirmishes between Catholics and Protestants. Protestants even fought among themselves. The theologies of Martin Luther, Ulrich Zwingli, and John Calvin diverged sharply on various points of the Lord's Supper.

Another famous controversy swirled around the Anabaptists and their claim that only believing adults could be baptized. Even if a person had been baptized as an infant, the Anabaptists said he or she must be rebaptized. Some Protes-

> The Roman Catholic Church claims seven sacraments: baptism, the Lord's Supper, penance, confirmation, marriage, ordination, and extreme unction. In contrast, Protestant churches recognize only the first two, because only these two are explicitly recorded in Scripture as having been instituted by Jesus himself.

tants reacted so strongly against this teaching that they killed Anabaptist Christians by drowning them in lakes and rivers. It was a horrible way of saying, "You want to be rebaptized by immersion? Here—get your fill of it!"

Most of us no longer argue with Anabaptists or debate the Mass with Roman Catholics. So we may be tempted to think that this section of the Catechism is a fossil of long-dead theological battles. Still, we can be grateful that the Catechism thoroughly discusses the sacraments, because this provides ample opportunity to reflect on baptism and communion.

INTIMATE AND PERSONAL

The theologian Augustine once called sacraments "visible words." Indeed, the Reformed tradition has always firmly held that the sacraments may never be cut off from the centrality of God's Word. That's why in most Protestant churches the pulpit stands in the middle, buttressed on either side by the baptismal font and the communion table. These sacraments stand next to God's Word—they are visible illustrations of the gospel.

Reformed confessional literature claims that God is personally active in the sacraments. Indeed, we are told that in the sacraments we meet God. Q&A 66 says that God himself uses the sacraments to seal his truths and promises to us. In this connection a footnote to Q&A 66 directs us to read Genesis 17 and its account of the Bible's first sacrament: circumcision.

This ritual was the sign of God's gracious covenant with Israel. Of course, circumcision was more than a mere physical sign. Its key significance was the deeper spiritual reality of a person's inward devotion to God. That is why in the Bible circumcision could also be a metaphor ("the circumcision of the heart"). But while the inward, spiritual reality was key, that did not mean that the physical sign was unimportant. As in our current sacraments, so in circumcision: the elements employed are significant. We may not substitute other elements, for we believe the ones given to us by God carry meaning.

In the case of circumcision we must ask why God would direct our attention to a body part that we generally conceal. Circumcision was a sacramental sign that could never be a mere theoretical practice—it touched a person too personally for that! This was a sacramental sign literally carved in a person's flesh, becoming a part of who that person is. Here was a sacrament so vivid, so real, so intensely personal that it touched a person's most private part.

Curiously, something of this same intimacy is true of the two sacraments we celebrate in the church today. These sacraments also touch our flesh in an intimate way. Babies and adults feel the water on their bodies—that's why we expect babies to squirm and squeal. When we participate in communion, we take something into our very bodies. Eating is an intensely personal act—we take what is outside us and bring it inside. The food and nutrients actually enter our bloodstream and course through the fabric of our being.

Through the sacraments we meet God in the totality of our beings—they involve us completely. But it's not magic or automatic. That was a key sticking point in the Reformation era. Catholics believed that the sacraments themselves delivered grace and salvation to people. Protestants claimed that the sacraments symbolized the grace and salvation already in a believer's heart. Peter Kreeft once put it this way: Catholics see the sacraments as doors, whereas Protestants see them as windows. Catholics believe that the sacraments are doors through which God's grace comes to a person. Protestants believe the sacraments are windows through which we view again the grace presented in the Bible and already in our hearts as a gift.

Though this is a helpful analogy, the picture may be a bit more complex. As we will soon see, we Protestants do affirm the active presence of God in the sacraments. The sacraments are not magic, they do not create salvation or grace or faith, but we believe they are more than just windows through which to watch God at work.

In the sacraments we meet God in a deeply spiritual way. Baptism and communion may be visual signs of the gospel, but they are also God's seal on that gospel—a seal God applies to us personally. So let us now turn to these two sacraments to see how and in what ways God meets us in the sacraments.

"The Reformed view of the sacraments is immediately evident in the references to 'signs and seals.' The focus of both sign and seal is 'the promise of the gospel.' Therefore, the sacraments cannot stand alone; the gospel or the preaching of the Word must always accompany them. As 'signs' the sacraments 'make us understand more clearly the promise of the gospel' and 'by our use of them' in faith, the Holy Spirit puts 'his seal on that promise.' The seal is there to guarantee and assure" (*A Mighty Comfort*, p. 73).

DROWNED AND REVIVED

John Timmer relates that a century ago in Ireland most people made their living in the fishing industry. The ocean was a source of life and livelihood. In those days fishermen wore heavy woolen sweaters with unique designs that varied from family to family. So Mr. McDonald always wore a pattern of black stripes against a red background; Mr. O'Malley wore a green sweater with yellow splotches. Far from being a simple fashion statement, these sweaters served a rather grim purpose. Each was different because these people knew that although the sea was the source of their life, it could also be a source of death. Sudden storms with huge swells could come upon the sea, tossing fishing boats like toys in a bathtub. When that happened, men died. Further, the rough, cold, brackish waters could so quickly decompose a person's body that by the time a drowning victim washed ashore he would be unrecognizable. That's why each family wore a different sweater: to identify their dead.

Water can be deadly. The people in biblical times knew this too. Of course, people in the Old and New Testaments certainly knew how vital water is for life, crops, and health. But they also feared water, viewing it as one of the two primal forces of evil or chaos, the other being the darkness of night. That is why in Genesis 1 God keeps water and darkness in check, separating water from dry land and light from darkness to carve out a safe niche for humanity where neither the seas nor the dark could harm them. In the Book of Revelation we are told that there will be no night and no sea in the New Creation. Chaos will be banished.

Water has the power both to give life and to take it. If we are truly to appreciate the sacrament of baptism, we need to remember both aspects of water. The Heidelberg Catechism points to two things seen in baptism: the water symbolizes our being washed, and the water symbolizes our being renewed.

First, as Q&A's 69 and 73 make clear, baptism is a spiritual washing every bit as real as the daily physical washings of our bodies. When you wash your hands after working in the garden, you can see the dirt swirl down the drain. Even so our spiritual "dirt" disappears through the inner cleansing of the Spirit. It is just that real.

But there is another important part of baptism—one which we usually overlook and one to which even the Catechism makes only passing reference in Q&A 70. A key meaning of the Greek word *baptizo*, "baptize," is "to drown." Indeed, this is one of the apostle Paul's favorite ways of thinking about baptism (as he does in Romans 6, a passage to which Q&A 70 directs our attention).

In baptism, we die—our old sinful selves are drowned. We emerge from baptism not just clean, but new. In the early days of the Christian church this was dramatically depicted at each baptism. On Easter Sunday all those who had passed through catechism class were baptized along with their children. The adults would strip off their clothes, be plunged under the water, and given new white robes as they emerged from the water. They had stripped off the old, pre-Christ person and had become a new person clothed with Christ himself.

In some churches today, whenever a baptism occurs, the minister follows up the actual baptism of the day by going up and down the aisles with an instrument that looks like a honey-dipper. He dips this into a bowl of water and then shakes out water onto the entire congregation. As he does so, he says, "Remember your baptism and be thankful." The idea is to remind each believer of his or her own baptism. Perhaps it happened to you as an infant, perhaps it happened later in life, but the point is that you must remember that once upon a time real water was splashed onto your body, vividly showing the reality of Jesus' blood washing your soul and so reminding you of the new kind of life you are to live every day.

As we noted above, the sacraments are supposed to be vivid, personal experiences that remind us of the vivid, personal touch of God's grace. Like a splash of cold water first thing in the morning, baptism jolts us and reminds us that a radical cleansing and a wholesale renewal have taken place. The waters of baptism have touched us—body and soul. It's that intimate, that personal, that real. Remember your baptism and be thankful!

> "Don't you know that all of us who were baptized into Christ Jesus were baptized into his death? We were therefore buried with him through baptism into death in order that, just as Christ was raised from the dead through the glory of the Father, we too may live a new life. If we have been united with him like this in his death, we will certainly also be united with him in his resurrection" (Rom. 6:3-5).

RARE DELICACIES

The film *Babette's Feast* tells a charming story of grace. Babette is a renowned French chef forced to flee Paris due to a political crisis. She lands in a tiny Danish village where she becomes the chief cook and bottle washer for two elderly sisters who head up an odd little religious community. These women know virtually nothing of Babette's past but are pleased with her meticulous cleanliness and her ability to make their simple peasant fare of beer bread and thin flounder soup.

After living in the village for some years, Babette discovers one day that she has won a lottery worth ten thousand francs. Out of love and gratitude for all they have done for her, Babette decides to use this money to cook a gourmet banquet for the sisters and their tiny congregation. So she sends to Paris for the finest of meats, vegetables, spices, china, stemware, wine, and cordials. In the end she spends her entire fortune to prepare a seven-course feast of stunning complexity and exquisite artistry.

But, alas, the meal's wonder is lost on all but one of the diners. Through a comedy of religious errors, the sisters become convinced that there is something spiritually amiss about the meal. They come to believe that enjoying the food would implicate them in some gross sin. Since they do not wish to hurt Babette's feelings, they and their congregation decide that they will eat but they will do so as though not eating. They will consume the food but will keep their minds focused on other topics.

So as the gourmet banquet proceeds, the church folks talk about anything but the food. Only one guest, a visiting soldier, is properly agog and sumptuously grateful for the rare delicacies placed before him. Whenever he mentions this to his fellow diners, they respond by commenting on the weather or on the current ocean conditions. They may as well have been consuming beer bread and flounder soup!

Still, something remarkable happens around Babette's banquet table. The tiny religious community had been plagued by strife and bickering, but as their conversation is fed by the fine food and lubricated by the fine drink, reconciliation begins to occur.

When the evening is finished, the congregation gathers under the stars to join hands and sing a hymn of praise. The sisters, grateful for this happy turn of events, marvel at what has happened. Somehow Babette's feast drew them back together. Only after their guests have left do the sisters discover what Babette has done and who she really is. Only then do they find that Babette is a world-class chef who had graciously spent her entire fortune on this rare meal. She could not return to Paris, for she had no resources left to do so. Never again would she exercise her gifts preparing such a meal. In the feast, Babette sacrificed her all.

When we gather around the holy banquet table of our Lord, do we understand and savor with gratitude what we're eating? Or do we sometimes eat in ignorance? Because of the mystery of it all, we will always be somewhat ignorant of its meaning. Still, we should try to understand as best we can the double feeding we receive. We should know that while our bodies are fed, our souls are also nourished in ways that draw us back toward our Lord and into deeper fellowship with each other.

IN REMEMBRANCE

In communion we fracture bread and spill wine to remember. In the Holy Supper we remember God's sacred history. We identify ourselves with the slain Lamb of God—we are reconnected to Calvary.

But why do we use bread and wine to do this? Why did our Lord choose the acts of eating and drinking to help us remember him? Surely Jesus could have given some other sign of remembrance. Why this one in particular?

There is nothing extraordinary about this food, after all. It's just simple bread and wine (see Q&A 78). And yet it represents a rich tradition. In the ancient world bread truly was the staff of life. It was a staple that every person ate every day. Bread was also the stuff of hospitality. Fresh bread was always offered to guests upon their arrival and at their departure. This latter bread was bread for the journey, or *waybread*. Bread bound a host and a guest together during the visit and after. They would break off bread from the one loaf and thus be knit together in fellowship.

Likewise, in the ancient world wine was viewed as a great gift of God. In fact, the Bible describes heaven as a place where there is a superabundance of good wine. That's why an extraordinary harvest of grapes in biblical times was considered a sign of God's favor and a foretaste of heaven.

When we hold the bread at the Lord's Table, we are holding the staff of life—it nourishes and sustains. It is waybread for the journey of life given to us by Jesus to bind us closer to himself. In fact, in a radical advance on the idea of binding together host and guest, the host who gives us this bread is giving us himself. The bread of communion is sometimes called "The Host" because this meal is not only hosted by Jesus; Jesus *is* the meal. Jesus is not merely sharing a common loaf; he has given and now shares his very self.

Somehow eating and drinking provide a quietly apt and striking metaphor for the intimacy involved in our union with Christ. As we noted above, eating is an intensely personal act, as we take what was outside us and bring it inside. But as Q&A's 75 and 79 say, that is precisely why it is so appropriate as a sacrament. We move from the undeniable texture of the bread on our tongue and the warming touch of the wine in our throat to the equally undeniable reality of Jesus feeding our souls with his self.

Q&A 76 even uses intimate language to describe this. The phrase "Flesh of his flesh and bone of his bone" is a clear echo of Genesis 2, where Eve is brought to Adam as his perfect physical and spiritual complement. Now this radical creation language is transferred to our union with Jesus through the Supper. This meal is a radical feeding and an intimate joining.

Like the tiny Danish congregation, we do not always understand what it is we're eating and how it is feeding our souls. But by God's Spirit, by the Host who has given his all, we are bound together with our Lord and with one another. When we get up from this table, when we receive this life, what should we do but gather under the stars, hand in hand, to sing our hymn of praise.

REFLECTIONS

▶ *Points to Ponder*

In the sacraments we meet God in a deeply spiritual way. Baptism and communion may be visual signs of the gospel, but they are also God's seal on that gospel—a seal God applies to us personally.

In baptism, we die—our old sinful selves are drowned. We emerge from baptism not just clean, but new.

When we gather around the holy banquet table of our Lord, do we understand and savor with gratitude what we're eating? Or do we sometimes eat in ignorance?

The bread of communion is sometimes called "The Host" because this meal is not only hosted by Jesus; Jesus is the meal.

▶ *Implications and Applications*

1. What did Augustine mean when he described the sacraments as "visible words"?

2. How do Protestants and Roman Catholics differ in their view of the sacraments?

3. What does the water of baptism symbolize? What happens to our spiritual dirt in baptism?

4. Why might it be good advice to "remember your baptism and be thankful"?

5. Describe how communion has been a "radical feeding and an intimate joining" in your own experience.

6. How has this unit enlarged your understanding of and love for the sacraments?

UNIT
FIVE

THE
DILEMMA
OF
GRACE

Author Philip Yancey once described two families of his acquaintance. One family was dominated by a mother and father who prescribed a rigid, almost legalistic, code of behavior for their children. Though it may go too far to say that these parents offered conditional love, they surely made it clear to their kids that good behavior would make acceptance by mom and dad much more likely. "Grace" was seldom heard in family devotions. Ironclad lists of biblical rules and regulations came up regularly. God, in these parents' presentation of him, was a strict monarch who demanded obedience or else.

The second family was gently led by parents who reveled in God's unconditional acceptance by grace alone and who attempted to embody this kind of love for their children. Though improper behavior was frowned on and confronted, such confrontations were loving and full of assurances that mom and dad's displeasure did not threaten their love. "Grace" was a word that came up routinely in table devotions. God, in their presentation of him, was seen best in Jesus' gracious and loving forgiveness of the sinners he met in his ministry.

Strikingly, however, Yancey notes that the children of the legalistic family grew into stable, happily married adults who are raising their kids in the Christian faith. The children of the second family, by way of unhappy contrast, have traveled in and out of difficulty: one daughter contracted AIDS through sexual promiscuity, a son has spent time both in jail and in drug rehabilitation clinics, still another daughter is in her fourth marriage.

Of course, many of us could tell similar stories with opposite endings. That is, we know legalistic parents whose children have reacted against their upbringing by shunning the church and engaging in rebellious behaviors. We also know grace-filled parents whose children have grown up to become healthy, strong, stable, and committed Christians.

Still, buried within Yancey's scenario is a seed of fear that many people harbor: namely, too much up-front grace, acceptance, and forgiveness can lead people to become morally slipshod. Some conclude that the only way to raise responsible children is to be very firm about what's right and wrong, severely punishing those who stray and rewarding those who toe the line. A swift restoration of the wayward child looks suspiciously like being "soft on sin."

This is also a theological concern. Does the Reformed insistence that salvation comes "by grace alone" make people indifferent to the moral life? The Heidelberg Catechism hammers away at legalism. We are told again and again that nothing we've done in the past and nothing we can ever do in the future will earn us entrance into God's kingdom. Once we are in the kingdom by grace, nothing we could ever do will exclude us. For if our deeds contributed to or detracted from our salvation in any way, we could not say that we are saved by grace alone.

So what keeps us from saying "Well then, let's live as we see fit. Let's eat, drink, and be merry since—even if we sin—it's covered!" The German thinker Heinrich Heine once cynically put it this way: "God likes to forgive. I like to sin. Really, the world is admirably arranged." What keeps us from thinking like Heine?

Can we Reformed people spend half our time trashing the importance of good works and then turn right around to spend the other half insisting that people perform good works anyway? Is that consistent?

DELIGHTING IN THE GOOD

Q&A 86 tackles this conundrum head on. If God pays our deeds no mind, why do we bother with good works? The answer says that we do good because in the process of saving us, God's grace also transforms us. His grace packs a powerful wallop. If the warhead of grace detonates at "ground zero" in our hearts, the shock waves of that explosion ripple into every nook and cranny of our existence, blowing away our sinfulness and bringing to life a New Creation.

In one of the Star Trek movies, a fictional scientist invents what she calls "Project Genesis." Genesis is essentially a bomb, but it is a bomb that destroys in order to make new. If the Genesis torpedo were detonated on the surface of a planet, a huge shock wave of energy would roar across the surface like a raging brush fire. But instead of blowing apart each object in its path, Genesis would gather up all the atoms and molecules and rearrange them into a preprogrammed matrix of new lifeforms.

By way of demonstration, Genesis is detonated on a moon that has no atmosphere and hence no water, plants, or life of any kind. As the Genesis wave burns across the surface, it first lays waste to the moon's craters, mountains, and dust. But then it immediately recombines those atoms and creates out of them a new world replete with a breathable atmosphere, green meadows, apple trees, and azure lakes teeming with fish.

This transforming effect is also implemented by God's grace. The power of Christ blows through our lives by the breath of the Holy Spirit, laying waste to what the Catechism calls "the old self" (Q&A's 88-89). The goal is not to destroy us, but to remake us. Grace takes the spiritual molecules of our souls and reassembles them into a "new self" that is designed

> "The catechism certainly echoes the gospel when it regards the good works which God requires of us as fruits of the Spirit's sanctifying work in a believer's heart. That perspective makes all the difference in the world. Christians who do not learn to distinguish good works of gratitude from good works of merit will be trapped in legalism. The line between the two is razor-thin, but all-important.   Understanding that there is absolutely nothing a believer can do for salvation because Christ has done it all makes one truly free to live the life of thanks. That was the great Protestant 'rediscovery'" (*A Mighty Comfort*, p. 95).

to be inhabited by God's Spirit. The Spirit then cultivates in us rich spiritual fruit and a heart fully oriented to God.

Of course, this does not mean that we are instantly immune to the lure of sin or that we will never commit a sin again in this life. What it does mean is that the fundamental orientation of our lives is in a Godward direction.

As Q&A 86 points out, a Godward life serves several wonderful functions. First, such a life gives God our deepest gratitude and praise. God is grieved when sin and evil sully his world. Recall the story of Noah and how God's heart was smitten with sorrow when he saw his "very good" Creation being ruined. Conversely, God is pleased when he sees things working the way he designed them to work.

If a father builds a tree house for his children, he takes great delight in seeing the joyful play of his kids—having fun is the best thanks they could give. How quickly the father's mood would change, however, if the kids did nothing but whine that it wasn't built right. How heavy this father's heart would be if the kids began to trash the tree house through rough and careless play.

God is thanked, praised, and delighted when people love and trust him enough to live in the world as God intended. But, the Catechism claims, good lives do still more. They demonstrate that there is indeed a holy power at work in us, and this fact assures us that our faith is real. What's more, when our neighbors see such a genuine transformation, they may become curious about God and his ways. Transformed lives can provide a gospel witness more compelling than that of words alone.

The Heidelberg Catechism reminds us of the great paradox of the gospel: we are not saved by good works, but neither are we saved without them. Good works and moral deeds may not be the root of our salvation, but they surely are the fruit that naturally appears as we come alive to the goodness of the world our loving God made.

Indeed, once we see the cross and recognize God's lavish love for us, we realize that everything God does for us is for our benefit. God designed us and this world for shalom—for mutually edifying relationships of wholeness and delight. It only makes sense that following God's designs leads us higher and deeper into just this kind of shalom.

To return to our tree-house analogy, no loving father would ever build a dangerous tree house for his children. When laying down some rules for how to play in it, a loving father would never suggest forms of play that would make falling or getting hurt more likely. Rather the father will design a sturdy tree house, and his rules will insure that the children will get maximum enjoyment at minimum risk.

According to the Catechism, the first part of leading a grateful, transformed life is trusting God enough to follow his loving design for this world—a design that is neatly sketched in the Ten Commandments.

LOVING THE LAW

Frederick Buechner observes that there are two kinds of laws. One kind tells us how things ought to be. A speed limit sign on the highway, for instance, declares how fast you should drive. This sign could, of course, be changed in the future, or you could break the law and drive faster. Still, the sign is there to tell you how you ought to drive on this stretch of road.

Another kind of law tells us not how things *ought* to be but rather how things *are*. The law of gravity for instance, tells us not that a hammer *should* fall when you let go of it, but that the hammer *will* fall. This is a law you can neither amend nor disobey. If you drive 70 in a 55 MPH zone, you may or may not suffer any consequences. However, even if you don't care for the law of gravity, letting go of a hammer that is poised over your foot will certainly result in some pain!

God's Law, Buechner says, is of this second type. Many people think that the Ten Commandments are arbitrary dictates of God—hoops God wants us to jump through for no particular reason. In reality, the Ten Commandments describe how things are. These are the main lines on God's creation blueprint. Staying within these lines, God says, will lead to our greatest beatitude in this world. We disobey these laws at our own risk.

The Ten Commandments are something like the blueprint of a house. If you decide to build a fireplace in your house, you would do well first to consult the blueprint. If the blueprint shows that the wall you want to knock out for a fireplace is a load-bearing wall, you would do well to heed that fact and leave the wall alone.

Few documents do a better job of bringing out the positive, life-affirming dimensions of God's Law than the Heidelberg Catechism. In the "Misery" unit of this study we noted the authors' strategic use of the summary of the Law in Q&A 4. We saw that by using Jesus' law of love, the Catechism cuts off the temptation to turn the Ten Commandments into a checklist for admission into God's kingdom.

The use of the full Ten Commandments in the third section of the Catechism is also strategic. Although the Commandments don't grant access into God's kingdom, they are the things you do once you enter that kingdom. Staying within the lines of God's design becomes the natural desire of our transformed hearts and a key way for us to thank and glorify God for all his mercies to us in Christ.

Placing the Law in the "Gratitude" section of the Catechism makes sense in another way as well. As a careful reading of the Old Testament makes clear—and as Paul points out in places like Romans and Galatians—God never intended for people to treat the Law as a how-to manual for salvation. Obeying the Law is always a response to God's salvation and grace and never something that brings salvation.

Think of ancient Israel. God did not come to Israel while it was in Egyptian slavery, issue the Ten Commandments, and say, "Now, my people, if you obey these ten laws, then I will consider rescuing you from Pharaoh's bondage." No, first God created a mighty nation of people to fulfill his gracious promise to Abraham. Then he swept his people out of Egypt with mighty deeds and an outstretched arm. Only after this salvation did the Law come. "This," God said, "is how you shall live after I have saved you."

The Israelites even came to see God's Law as a gift, which at first sounds odd. Few parental statements can more quickly baffle a child than the one that goes something like, "We've made these rules because we love you. They are for your own

---

The Catechism picks up on three separate uses of God's Law that have traditionally been identified by Protestant theologians:

- **The civic use provides the basis and guide for ordering and maintaining justice in society as a whole (see Q&A 105).**

- **As our teacher of sin, it shows us how far we fall short of meeting God's just requirements of us, leading us to Christ, who alone can justify us (see Q&A's 3-5).**

- **As our guide to gratitude, it shows us how we can genuinely live lives of gratitude to God for the salvation we receive in Christ.**

good." To a child, rules seem to spoil the fun; yet parents act like they are doing their kids a favor by making up rules.

Israel recognized that God's rules really were a gift for her own benefit. Thus the psalmist could often sing out, "How I love your law, O Lord!" He recognized that through the Law, God had let his people in on the secrets of this world. God had shown them how to live in ways that would make them happy and blessed in their marriages, in families, and in society. Such knowledge is a gift!

BROAD, DEEP, AND POSITIVE

A key characteristic of the Catechism's presentation of the Law is the marvelous way that it broadens, deepens, and positively applies the commandments. Far from letting us believe that the Ten Commandments are a series of narrow "don'ts," the Catechism shows that the true glory of God's Law is the things it permits us to do.

Let's look at a few examples. Note how the Catechism broadens the range of the commandments. "Taking God's name in vain" includes not only blasphemous cursing but also perjury, empty oaths, and even being silent bystanders when others do these things. Sabbath rest does not apply only to the seventh day but includes a seven-day-a-week "resting" from sin. Honoring our fathers and our mothers means obeying also "all those in authority over me."

The Catechism also deepens the true meaning of these laws. "Murder" includes the seeds of murder—hatred, envy, anger, vindictiveness—as well as murder-like deeds such as hurling insults, cooking up murderous images in our minds, and even giving dirty looks. Similarly the law against adultery includes—as Jesus made clear—fantasies of the heart, leering looks, and thoughts that make other people into sexual objects. Stealing includes the obvious things such as swiping a pack of gum from the store, but it also includes the roots of theft, chief among which is greed.

Finally, the Catechism does an outstanding job of applying each of these commandments in a positive way. We are not to worship idols, but we are to embrace God in every way. We are not to kill, insult, or belittle our neighbors, but we are to love them and protect them from all harm. We are not to steal from or swindle our neighbors, but we are to treat them fairly and share with them out of our own abundance. We are not to besmirch someone's reputation with lies, but we are to guard and advance our neighbor's good name.

These patterns represent the rhythms of the grateful life and the natural desires of the transformed heart. All such ways of living please God, who thoroughly enjoys seeing us live life the way it was meant to be lived. Even if there are times when we feel the sinful tug to make up our own rules and do things our own way, sticking with God's designs shows God that we entrust him with our lives. Such loving trust and willing obedience—created and fueled in us by God's Spirit—are indeed, in God's eyes, a most elegant "thank you" for all his mercy to us.

Q&A's 94-113 first inform us what each of the Ten Commandments tell us *not* to do; then they tell us what we *should* do. This pattern clearly reaches back to Q&A 88: "What is involved in genuine repentance? Two things: the dying away of the old self, and the coming-to-life of the new." Page back to Q&A's 88-90 to discover how tightly the Catechism has structured this section on Gratitude.

R E F L E C T I O N S

▶ *Points to Ponder*

Once we are in the kingdom by grace, nothing we could ever do will exclude us. For if our deeds contributed to or detracted from our salvation in any way, we could not say that we are saved by grace alone.

If the warhead of grace detonates at "ground zero" in our hearts, the shock waves of that explosion ripple into every nook and cranny of our existence, blowing away our sinfulness and bringing to life a New Creation.

Grace takes the spiritual molecules of our souls and reassembles them into a "new self" that is designed to be inhabited by God's Spirit. The Spirit then cultivates in us rich spiritual fruit and a heart fully oriented to God.

The Heidelberg Catechism reminds us of the great paradox of the gospel: we are not saved by good works, but neither are we saved without them.

The Ten Commandments describe how things are. These are the main lines on God's creation blueprint. Staying within these lines, God says, will lead to our greatest beatitude in this world. We disobey these laws at our own risk.

Sticking with God's designs shows God that we entrust him with our lives. Such loving trust and willing obedience—created and fueled in us by God's Spirit—are indeed, in God's eyes, a most elegant "thank you" for all his mercy to us.

▶ *Implications and Applications*

1. How would your upbringing compare with the two families described at the beginning of this unit? To what degree did "grace" play a role in your childhood home? How have your early experiences with grace—or lack thereof—affected your view of grace now?
2. Why do Christians do good works?
3. What relation, if any, do good works have to salvation?
4. Why do questions about the Ten Commandments appear in the "Gratitude" section of the Catechism?
5. How has this unit broadened your understanding of the purpose of the Ten Commandments?

UNIT
SIX

GRATEFUL REQUESTS

A few years ago *Newsweek* magazine ran a cover story on prayer. According to a poll taken in the United States, 91 percent of women and 85 percent of men say they pray at least once a week. More than 50 percent of both men and women claim to pray at least once a day. What's more, publishers say that books on prayer sell extremely well—there are now more than two thousand titles on the market dealing with various aspects of prayer. Despite our highly scientific technological age, prayer is a hot topic.

The *Newsweek* article also notes that most people use prayer for personal enhancement. Most say they generally pray for God to give them something—usually something material. Others praise the act of prayer because it strengthens their inner being. One expert said that a good sex life combined with a good prayer life may be the formula for a successful marriage.

While these views focus only on the pray-er, the Catechism shifts the focus to God. Q&A 116 says that "prayer is the most important part of the thankfulness God requires of us." How might that be? How does the act of praying thank God?

After all, many of our own prayers are petitionary—we seek something from God. Many of us were taught to remember the four parts of prayer through the acronym ACTS: adoration, confession, thanksgiving, supplication. But if we are honest, we must admit that many of our prayers skip directly to supplication: we urgently ask God to keep our children safe as they go off to school in the morning, to give us a favorable lab report, to help our presentation before the boss to go well, to heal the rift in a friendship.

> *Adoration* means that we give honor, glory, and praise to God for who God is and for what God does. *Confession* is our humble, frank, and honest relating to God of the things we should have done and didn't, and the things we did that we shouldn't have. *Thanksgiving* refers to the parts in our prayer in which we verbalize our gratitude to God. *Supplication* expresses our dependency on God as we ask God to provide for the needs of others and for ourselves.

Of course, the Catechism reflects Jesus' teaching that all such requests are proper. Q&A 118 asks what God commands us to pray for, and the answer comes back: *"Everything* we need, spiritually and physically" [emphasis added]. Still, how do our requests thank God?

Imagine you had a son who, seven days a week, kept asking for things. "Mom and Dad, I want this, please get me that, could I please have this, pleeease?" Would we look at such a child and conclude that he is a really grateful kid? Would each subsequent request add to our sense that he's a thankful little boy at heart? Probably not.

We would be more likely to say that a child who rarely asked for anything, who was thrilled at the least little gift, who freely and often told his parents how much he loved them, was truly grateful. So why would we regard the one who keeps on asking and requesting day in and day out as being grateful?

In God's sight, even petitionary prayers count as expressions of thanks. Why? Because they are a fitting response to the grandeur and grace of God. The very act of coming to God, of placing a request before him, shows our confidence in God. For instance, if your son comes to you with a problem or request, you feel gratified that he trusted you enough to bring it to your attention. He could have kept quiet about it, he could have gone to his friends—but he didn't. He came to you. He saw in you some wisdom, some ability to solve this problem or grant this request. The very act of bringing it to you and not to someone else is itself a good thing.

So the Catechism reflects a biblical irony: the more needs and wants we entrust to God's providence and mercy, the more God is praised and thanked. Asking God for help is a statement of our faith in his ability to help.

Such prayers, like the desire to keep God's Law, rise up in us as a natural, inevitable result of our having been saved by grace in Christ Jesus the Lord. When we have the Holy Spirit living in our hearts, we are naturally bent Godward. The posture of our lives inclines toward God, so that it is natural—and for God it is wonderful—that we should bring everything to him.

Of course, a proper prayer life includes more than requests. As Q&A 117 reminds us, when we come before God in prayer, we see and praise God's unspeakable grandeur and power. When we see how holy God is, we see all over again how unholy we are in our sin and misery. This reminds us that if it were not for Jesus, we would have no right to expect God to listen to us. In fact, without Jesus, in whose Name we pray, we would have no access to God at all. (That's why the closing words "For Jesus' sake" should not be said lightly. Those words are our constant reminder of the One whose shed blood and ongoing grace makes it possible for us to pray and be heard.)

"Prayer is the hallmark of the believer. One who has been born from above can no more live without prayer than the natural man can live without oxygen. For what, after all, is prayer? It is fundamentally the longing aspiration of the regenerate heart for the true God as [its] portion" (G. I. Williamson, *The Heidelberg Catechism,* p. 209).

True Christian prayer wells up from the depths of our hearts when those hearts become the dwelling place of the Spirit. True prayer recognizes and praises God for what he is and does. True prayer includes confessing our sin and seeking God's forgiving mercy. True prayer thanks God for his mercy even in the midst of petition.

TEACH US TO PRAY

As we noted in Unit 1, the Catechism's authors sought always to be biblical. So rather than be abstract in discussing prayer, Ursinus, Olevianus, and company picked the New Testament's premiere prayer as their starting point. When the disciples asked Jesus, "Teach us to pray," Jesus responded with what we now call "The Lord's Prayer." Ever since that time, this prayer has been memorized, spoken, and studied because it contains the essence of true prayer. In addition to being prayed word for word, many have also recognized, as does the Catechism, that this prayer is a model on which to base our own prayers to God.

The Catechism's treatment of the prayer is compact and fairly brief. Following an explanation of the opening words, "Our Father in heaven" (Q&A's 120-121), the remainder of the prayer is divided into six requests, each of which receives just one question and answer (Q&A's 122-127). The Catechism then comments on the concluding lines which, though apparently not originally spoken by Jesus, have traditionally been appended to the prayer ("For yours is the kingdom and the power and the glory forever, Amen").

> The reason that the concluding phrase of the Lord's Prayer appears in the King James Version of Matthew 6:13 and not in later versions is that the KJV based its translation on later copies of this gospel than did subsequent versions. These words crept into the text during the ninth century. Earlier versions did not have them. Most Bible scholars assume that the earlier copies more likely reflect the original.

Like its treatment of the Ten Commandments, the Heidelberger unpacks each line of the prayer carefully and thoughtfully in order to deepen our understanding of these familiar words. It makes clear, for instance, that the first three requests—for the hallowing of God's name, the coming of God's kingdom, and the doing of God's will—are all radical requests that should result in radical obedience.

Q&A 122 asserts that to hallow or bless the name of our triune God means that we will not only worship God for all his works, but we will seek his direction in all that we think, do, and say. Long after we've said "Amen" and have risen from our knees, our prayers keep influencing us. Likewise, praying for the coming kingdom and the doing of God's will implies a desire to live counter-cultural lives in this sinful world. It implies living in such a way that the ways of God's kingdom are obvious to those around us.

In other words, the Catechism reflects the old Latin adage *Ora et Labora,* "Pray and Work." If we truly believe that the God to whom we pray is the God whose victory in Christ is real and whose kingdom has already begun to break into this world, then we must live out our prayers in all that we do. Our prayers not only praise God, they also change us.

Many people seem to see prayer as a substitute for action. At the end of Bertolt Brecht's play *Mother Courage and Her Children,* a farmer, his wife, and a mute girl named Kattrin witness a regiment of armed soldiers silently closing in on a neighboring village. As they realize that slaughter is imminent, the farmer and his wife say, "What can we do!? Oh, if only there were more of us, perhaps we could do something to help or warn the villagers. But there's absolutely nothing we can do! So let's pray. Our Father, who art in heaven, hear our prayer! Protect the people in the village."

But while the couple is praying, the mute girl Kattrin slips away, grabs a drum, climbs onto the roof of the farmhouse, and begins to bang the drum loudly as a warning to the village. Horrified, the couple begs her to stop lest she bring some trouble on them. But Kattrin continues to bang away until finally a soldier shoots her dead.

Prayer does not come off very well in this scene. It's a last resort, and a rather safe one at that. Because the farmer and his wife could do nothing, they prayed. No one would have shot them for that; compared to what Kattrin did, their prayer was no threat. Prayer, many people think, is what you do when all else fails. Or it's something you do when you don't dare to do anything else. Either way, if you could or would do something else, you wouldn't pray. Unhappily, as with the farm couple in the play, Christians sometimes affirm this kind of thinking. As someone once wrote, when people asked Christians in Europe what they had done to help the Jews during Hitler's Holocaust, the most deceitful answer they gave was, "We prayed for them."

Some people seem to believe prayer is a flight from reality and responsibility. But the Catechism shows that prayer is our starting point for a deep and holy engagement *with* reality. We pray for the integrity and holiness of God's name and kingdom so that the Holy Spirit can goad us to do holy acts consistent with God's holy kingdom. As Q&A 123 says, when we pray "Your kingdom come," we are asking God to "destroy the Devil's work . . . [and] every force which revolts against you . . . until your kingdom is so complete and perfect that you are all in all." But though all of this is indeed God's work, prayer reminds us that he accomplishes it through us.

PRAYING FOR THE REAL WORLD

In one of the many poignant sections of C. S. Lewis's *The Screwtape Letters,* the senior demon Screwtape advises his nephew Wormwood how to tempt a new Christian even when he is praying. "Make sure he always prays for things that are very 'spiritual,' that he is always concerned with the state of his mother's soul but never with her rheumatism. I have had patients so well in hand that they could be turned at a moment's notice from the impassioned prayer for a wife or son's soul to beating or insulting the real wife and son without a qualm. It is funny how mortals always picture us as putting things *into* their minds when in reality we mostly must keep things *out.*"

The Catechism asserts the biblical truth that we are to pray for all things, be they spiritual or physical. We are to pray in the real world for the real world. We are to pray from the midst of our real, day-to-day lives for our real, day-to-day lives and for the struggles, concerns, lapses, and issues that our lives encompass.

The last three requests of the Lord's Prayer highlight this fact. The Catechism expands the request for "daily bread" to command us to pray for our every need. Doing so reminds us of our utter dependence on God, that God is "the source of everything good" and that were it not for his daily blessing, none of our work, toil, fret, money, or worry would do us any good.

God and God alone is our providential Provider. We may receive our daily bread through many different sources and from the toil of many different hands, but it is finally God's hand that we must see behind it all. As Martin Luther once commented, when a family gathers at the breakfast table to pray "Give us this day our daily bread," God is at that moment busy answering their request as the baker across town pulls the day's first loaves from the oven.

We are also directed to reflect on another daily reality: our sin and the sins of others. To hide our sins from God is foolish. But to seek God's forgiveness while not forgiving other people's sins against us is, according to Jesus, more than foolish—it is evidence that we don't understand God's grace. By grace alone God has freely forgiven us for the enormous debt of our sins. We are now obligated to turn around and forgive others their comparatively puny debts to us. Q&A 125 says we must be "fully determined" to forgive others as a natural result of the grace of God in our lives.

The Catechism concludes its treatment of the Lord's Prayer with a request for God to shore us up in the face of temptation as we travel the road to God's complete kingdom victory. This leads naturally into the closing words, which attribute to God the kingdom, power, and glory forever.

KEEPING AT IT

Of course, prayer is not always easy. There are times when we feel spiritually dry and barren—when we sense a certain dullness to our prayers. Sometimes our prayers come slowly, if at all. Perhaps we are recovering from a grievous loss. Perhaps something in our life is blocking our prayers, making them seem like whistling in the dark. Perhaps our prayers seem mundane and predictable. Shouldn't something exciting happen to us if we have a "good" prayer life?

Not necessarily. If it is true, as an old hymn puts it, that "as I breathe I pray," then our prayer life is our biography. God knows that life has its ups and downs—so does our prayer life. God knows that our lives are not always filled with spiritual excitement. We should not expect our prayer life to be constantly scintillating either.

In the New Testament, especially in his parables, Jesus never promised that prayer would be easy. He counsels that we keep at it, that we be persistent and insistent, that we not give up. Persistence is difficult in the valleys of life. But if we can live those moments in God's presence, then perhaps our anguished silences, our tear-streaked faces, even our clenched fists beating on the walls of life can themselves be a kind of prayer. Our God, who knows and understands us intimately, hears the prayers we cannot utter just as surely as the ones we can.

Even when we are not in a valley, prayer can seem more like a duty than a joy. The Catechism realizes that such days will come—that's why it avoids making prayer into a gush of emotions. Rather, we are told that we must pray, that we are commanded to pray regardless of our feelings on a given day.

C. S. Lewis once observed that God is pleased even when we must make a deliberate effort to pray. Prayer is a duty for us, but it's not a grim one—it is a daily obligation on a par with

Kuyvenhoven asks: "If, then, on the one hand, the various trials and tests of this life are a necessary part of our earthly training and if, on the other hand, God himself places his children (Abraham, the people of Israel, Jesus, and everyone God loves) in a position where Satan may attack them, why should we even ask *not* to be led into temptation?"

He then offers this answer: "Because only fools would rush in where even Jesus feared to tread. Sometimes the commander has to send his troops into battle. When he does so, the soldiers know that there is no other way to peace than through this war. But only those who do not know the perils of war desire the battle" (*Comfort and Joy*, p. 309).

> Prayer does not always need to come with deep emotion. But it must always be genuine. In his commentary on the Heidelberg Catechism, Herman Veldkamp observes that the third commandment is probably broken more often in church than in the bar. Thoughtless, formalistic worship dishonors God as much as cursing and swearing over empty beer glasses.

eating and drinking. We need to make prayer a routine part of our daily lives so that we miss it in the same manner we would miss a meal—with hunger pangs and an empty rumbling in our souls.

In its closing words, the Catechism reminds us that God is near to us and attentive to us even more than we are to him. God is with us and communes with us even more than we have a desire to commune with him. In its explanation of the little word "Amen," we are told that "it is even more certain that God listens to my prayer than that I really desire what I pray for."

These words take us beyond emotional states and into the abiding presence of our Lord. This final question and answer rounds out the entire Heidelberg Catechism for "Amen" means "This is sure to be!" This fitting end to the Catechism tells us that the truths contained in this entire document are likewise "sure to be!" Given the deeply personal, pastoral, and pious tone of the Heidelberg Catechism, it is only fitting that the words of these 129 questions and answers be recited prayerfully and concluded with a resounding "Amen—all of this is sure to be! Hallelujah! Amen."

REFLECTIONS

▶ *Points to Ponder*

In God's sight, even petitionary prayers count as expressions of thanks. Why? Because they are a fitting response to the grandeur and grace of God.

This prayer has been memorized, spoken, and studied because it contains the essence of true prayer. In addition to being prayed word for word, many have also recognized, as does the Catechism, that this prayer is a model on which to base our own prayers to God.

To hallow or bless the name of our triune God means that we will not only worship God for all his works, but we will seek his direction in all that we think, do, and say.

The Catechism shows that prayer is our starting point for a deep and holy engagement with reality.

We are to pray in the real world for the real world.

Jesus never promised that prayer would be easy. He counsels that we keep at it, that we be persistent and insistent, that we not give up.

▶ *Implications and Applications*

1. What might account for the huge interest in prayer today?
2. How do our requests serve to thank and praise God?
3. Why do people sometimes turn to prayer as "a last resort"? What does this say about their view of prayer?
4. In what ways does prayer engage reality?
5. What are the elements of a good prayer life? What hinders your prayer life? What can you do to overcome those hindrances?
6. How has this unit enlarged your understanding of the importance of prayer?